Jessica's Skateboard

Written by Simon Crosbie

Illustrated by Teresa Culkin-Lawrence

sundance

 a black dog book

Published by
Sundance Publishing
P.O. Box 1326
234 Taylor Street
Littleton, MA 01460

Copyright © text Simon Crosbie
Copyright © illustrations Teresa Culkin-Lawrence

First published 2000 by
Pearson Education Australia Pty. Limited
95 Coventry Street
South Melbourne 3205 Australia
Exclusive United States Distribution: Sundance Publishing

ISBN 0-7608-5017-8

Printed in China

Contents

Chapter One

The Coolest Skateboard _____ 1

Chapter Two

The Double Twist _____ 5

Chapter Three

The Plan _____ 9

Chapter Four

"Gotcha!" _____ 19

Chapter Five

Perfect _____ 25

Characters

Jessica loves
trying new tricks
on her skateboard.

Sam is a
skateboarder too,
but he's not as good
as Jessica.

Chapter One

The Coolest Skateboard

Jessica was the best skateboarder
on the block. She had the coolest
skateboard. She had saved all year
to buy it.

Her best friend was Sam.

He was a cool skateboarder, too.

Every day they practiced on the ramp

with other kids from the block.

Jessica's best trick was a full twist.

She dreamed of doing a double twist.

Sam wanted to do a double twist, too.

Chapter Two
The Double Twist

The day Jessica was ready to try a double
twist, everyone gathered to cheer her on.
She skated down the ramp.
She flew through the air.

As she started to spin, her skateboard
shot out from under her. It raced down
the sidewalk and through the gate.
Jessica and Sam ran after it. It sped away.

Jessica's skateboard zipped down the street
until it disappeared.

Chapter Three
The Plan

Jessica was miserable. It would be months
before she could save enough money
for a new skateboard.

Suddenly, she had an idea.
Sam could try the trick!

When the skateboard took off,
the kids would be ready to follow it.
When it raced down the street,
they could watch where it went.

Jessica told Sam the plan.

"What?" said Sam, "You want me
to lose my skateboard, too?"

"No," said Jessica. "I want you to try
a double twist."

"Do you think you can do it, Sam?"
asked Jessica. "Then we can follow
your skateboard."

Sam thought for a moment.
"Yes," said Sam. "I'm sure I can."

The next day, everyone was ready.

Sam did everything Jessica had done.

He skated down the ramp and jumped.

The skateboard landed in a flower bed.

The second time, Sam landed
on his bottom. The skateboard landed
in his lap.

The third time, Sam flew as high as he
could and started to spin. The skateboard
zoomed out from under him.

The kids were ready.

They held up a sign for Jessica's grandpa,

who was watching for the skateboard.

The sign said, "Skateboard coming."

Grandpa waved to Grandma.

"Quick!" said Jessica. "Start the car, Grandma."

Chapter Four
"Gotcha!"

Grandma and Jessica followed the
skateboard down a tree-lined street.

They followed it over a bridge.

They watched as it rolled into a
dead-end street.

"Gotcha!" said Jessica.

They hurried down the street.
At the end, there was a huge
Smith Company dumpster.
But there was no sign of the skateboards.

"The skateboards have disappeared,"
said Jessica.

"It's a mystery," said Grandma.

Jessica stared at the dumpster.
"I think I know where they are," she said.

Chapter Five
Perfect

Jessica called the Smith Company.
The next day, Mr. Smith used
a huge truck to move the dumpster.
The skateboards were there.

"Yes!" said Jessica.

Jessica and Sam still go to the ramp
to do their tricks. Now they make sure
that they close the gate before they start.

After 36 tries, Jessica finally
did a perfect double twist.
Sam is still trying.